My Sk...

Maxine Rose

Illustrated by Randol Eagles

Dominie Press, Inc.

This is my new skateboard. My uncle gave it to me for my birthday.

This is my new helmet. My mom gave it to me for my birthday.

These are my new knee pads. My dad gave them to me for my birthday.

These are my new elbow pads.
My grandma gave them to me
for my birthday.

Before I ride my skateboard I have to put on my helmet, my knee pads, and my elbow pads.

Now I can hardly walk.

But on my skateboard
I can fly!